Approaches
to **writing**
and **language**

BOOK 2

Sheila Lane
& Marion Kemp

Approaches
to **writing**
and **language**

BOOK 2

Ward Lock Educational
A MEMBER OF THE LING KEE GROUP

Ling Kee

WARD LOCK EDUCATIONAL CO., LTD.
T. R. House, 1 Christopher Road,
East Grinstead, Sussex RH19 3BT.

A member of the Ling Kee Group
LONDON · HONG KONG · NEW YORK · SINGAPORE

First published 1980
Reprinted 1981, 1982, 1984, 1985, 1987, 1989

Designed by Clare Osborn
Illustrated by David Mostyn and Tony Morris
Set in 14 point Futura and Stymie

Approaches to Writing and Language

Book 1   0 7062 3926 1
Book 2   0 7062 3927 X
Book 3   0 7062 3928 8
Book 4   0 7062 3929 6

Printed in Hong Kong

Contents

Did you know . . . _____ 6

Stars _____ 9

The Two Magicians _____ 12

Funny folk _____ 13

Fireworks and flashes _____ 16

All kinds of weather _____ 20

The Kingdom of Greyland _____ 22

Christmas _____ 25

A Walk in the Dark _____ 28

Country creatures _____ 32

What in the world? _____ 34

You never can tell _____ 36

Faces _____ 38

The wicked one _____ 40

Talking with pictures _____ 42

The hot hatful _____ 45

Friends _____ 46

Making a choice _____ 48

Thinking about food _____ 50

Trouble in the Ark _____ 54

Picture poems and shape poems _____ 58

Sail away _____ 60

Acknowledgments _____ 64

Did you know . . . that totem poles were made by some North American Indian tribes?

This totem pole belonged to The Great Chief of The Thunderbirds.

The Thunderbirds were sometimes called The Birds-of-the-Air.

The rings showed that this chief was very important.

The wooden pole was covered with paintings and carvings. These showed some of the brave deeds of the chief's ancestors.

The woman is holding two rattles which she used for calling whales out of the sea.

Write

Write about: *The Chief's Totem Pole*

Begin by filling in the missing words from the information.

Once there was a tribe of North American Indians called The _____ .
Sometimes The Thunderbirds were called The _____-_____-_____-_____ .
The chief's totem pole was covered with _____ and _____ .

Write some more about Chief Thunderbird's totem pole.

Kam made his own totem pole by painting pictures and signs on empty cartons. Then he stuck the cartons together. You can find out about Kam by looking at his totem pole before you read his writing.

Kam's totem

Kam's writing

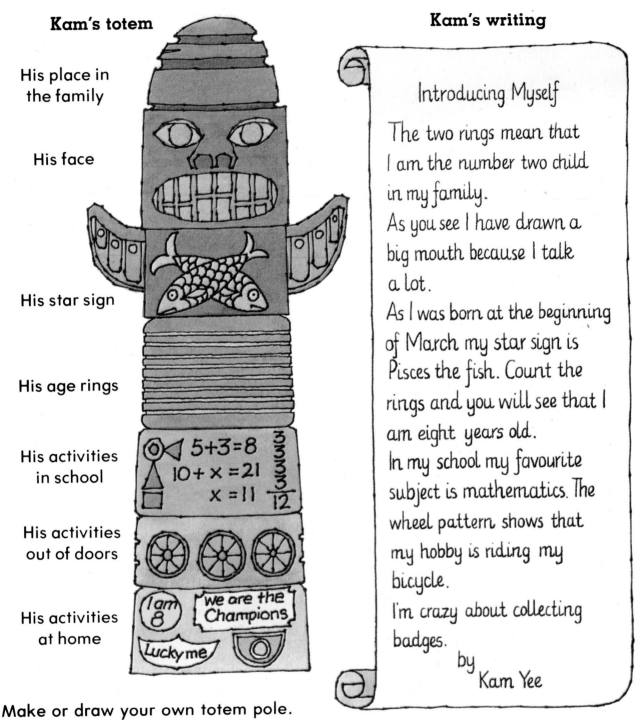

His place in the family

His face

His star sign

His age rings

His activities in school

His activities out of doors

His activities at home

Introducing Myself

The two rings mean that I am the number two child in my family.

As you see I have drawn a big mouth because I talk a lot.

As I was born at the beginning of March my star sign is Pisces the fish. Count the rings and you will see that I am eight years old.

In my school my favourite subject is mathematics. The wheel pattern shows that my hobby is riding my bicycle.

I'm crazy about collecting badges.

by Kam Yee

Make or draw your own totem pole.

Write

Write a description of yourself.

Ask your friends to say what all the pictures and signs on your totem pole mean before you let them read your writing.

7

You can find out more about Kam by reading his diary.
Kam wrote notes on his 'jotter' calendar.

October

2 Monday   Dentist 4 pm
3 Tuesday   Take back library books
4 Wednesday Write letter to Uncle John in America
5 Thursday   Zoo - take sandwiches to school
6 Friday   Cat's birthday
7 Saturday   Club - 11 am
8 Sunday   Tea with Granny

Kam wrote his diary each day.

Monday 2nd October

When I woke up the sun was shining through my window and I felt happy. Then I remembered that I had to go to the dentist. School seemed to go slowly because I kept thinking about the dentist. But I only had one small filling and that did not hurt. On the way back on the bus Mum gave me 20p.

Tuesday 3rd October

Make your own 'jotter' calendar for a whole week.
The notes are to remind you about important happenings on each day.

Write your own diary

Write your own diary for: *A Whole Week of My Life*

Stars

Do you know this old rhyme?

Monday's child is fair of face,
Tuesday's child is full of grace,
Wednesday's child is full of woe,
Thursday's child has far to go,
Friday's child is loving and giving,
Saturday's child works hard for his living,
But the child that is born on the Sabbath day
Is blithe and bonny, good and gay.

Were you born on a lucky day?

Do you have a lucky star?

Look at these lucky stars and think about
the ones you would like to have.

a visitor

a letter

new clothes to wear

a surprise present

a new pet

extra pocket money

an invitation

a holiday

a new friend

a journey

If you could have a whole week of lucky days,
which stars would you choose?

Write

My Lucky Star Week

Monday brought _____ .
Tuesday brought _____ .

The Strange Star

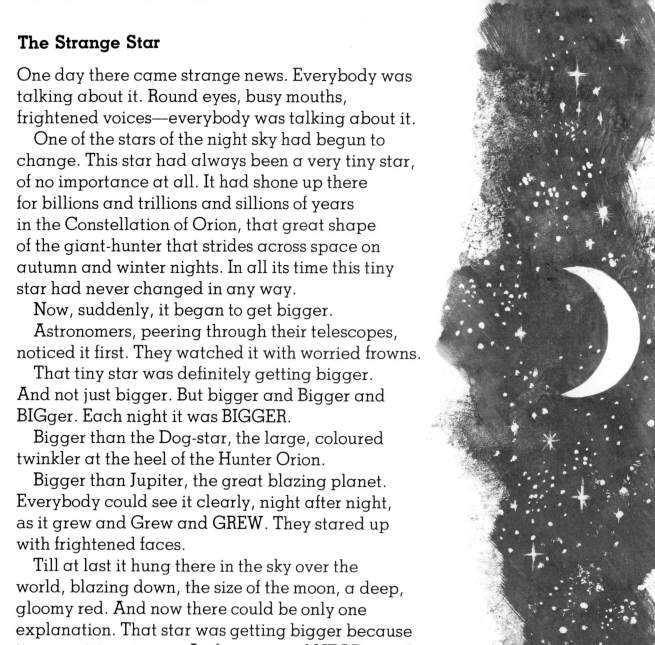

One day there came strange news. Everybody was talking about it. Round eyes, busy mouths, frightened voices—everybody was talking about it.

One of the stars of the night sky had begun to change. This star had always been a very tiny star, of no importance at all. It had shone up there for billions and trillions and sillions of years in the Constellation of Orion, that great shape of the giant-hunter that strides across space on autumn and winter nights. In all its time this tiny star had never changed in any way.

Now, suddenly, it began to get bigger.

Astronomers, peering through their telescopes, noticed it first. They watched it with worried frowns.

That tiny star was definitely getting bigger. And not just bigger. But bigger and Bigger and BIGger. Each night it was BIGGER.

Bigger than the Dog-star, the large, coloured twinkler at the heel of the Hunter Orion.

Bigger than Jupiter, the great blazing planet. Everybody could see it clearly, night after night, as it grew and Grew and GREW. They stared up with frightened faces.

Till at last it hung there in the sky over the world, blazing down, the size of the moon, a deep, gloomy red. And now there could be only one explanation. That star was getting bigger because it was getting nearer. And nearer and NEARer and NEARER.

Ted Hughes

Imagine that you are looking up at the night sky
and you see a gigantic star rushing towards the earth.
Out of the star flies the strangest creature
you have ever seen.
As it comes nearer, NEARer, NEARER, make up a
name for it from some of these shapes.

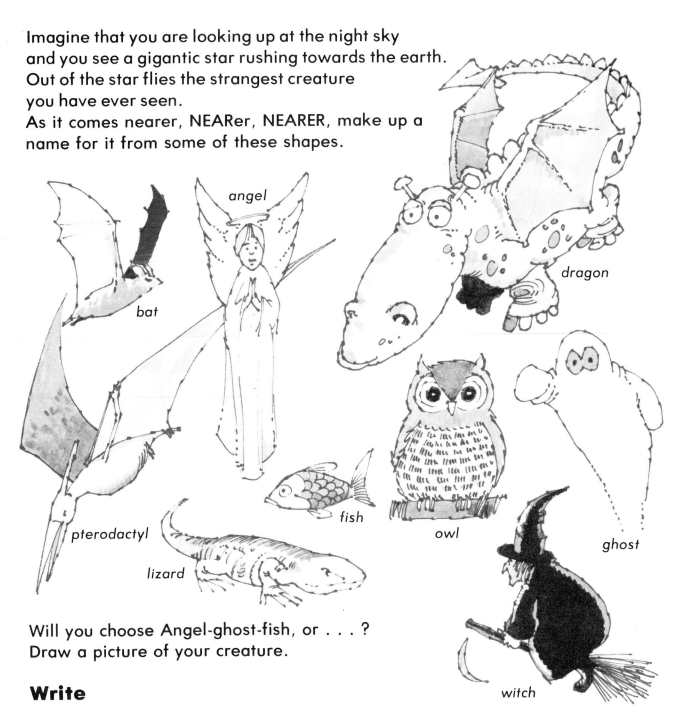

angel

bat

dragon

pterodactyl

fish

owl

ghost

lizard

witch

Will you choose Angel-ghost-fish, or . . . ?
Draw a picture of your creature.

Write

Write these headings:

Animal Food	**Plant Food**	**Metal Food**
meat	grass	tin cans

Write more foods your creature might be looking
for under each heading.

Think about what your creature's giant voice might say
as it rumbles round the world towards you.

Write your own story

You could call your writing: *The Creature from the Night Sky*

The Two Magicians

These pictures tell a story about two magicians.

Look again

Look again at the first magician's hand when he turns water into ice.
Which hand is he using when he changes the ice back into water?

Write your own story

You could call your writing: *Finger Magic* or: *Right Hand . . . Left Hand*

Funny folk

Look at this Strange Man.

He is made with some of the shapes on the page.

Which of these mathematical shapes are used
for the Strange Man?

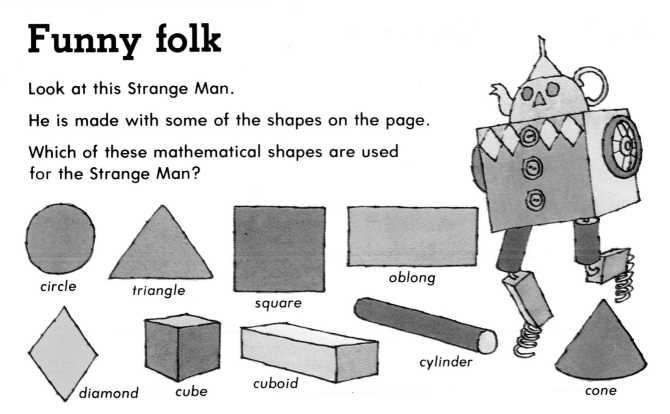

circle   triangle   square   oblong   cylinder

diamond   cube   cuboid   cone

Which of these 'bits and pieces' are used for the Strange Man?

funnel   wire   colander   balloon   rope

egg box   wheel   milk bottle top   button   metal teapot

Draw or make your own Strange Man.

Think of some more 'bits and pieces' for his body parts.

Here are the names of **five body parts:**

| eyes | teeth | hands | ears | feet |

How will you make these body parts for your Strange Man?

Write

Write about:

My Strange Man

For eyes I use _____ .
For teeth _____ .
For _____ .

13

Think about ways of naming body parts.
Think about words which describe what the part does.

Teeth are for eating.
Teeth can be called eaters or choppers or . . .

Here are some body parts.

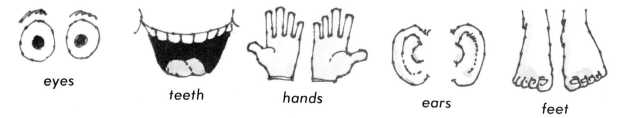

eyes   teeth   hands   ears   feet

Here are some words which can describe body parts.

| chewers | touchers | lookers | kickers | hearers |

Match one word to each body part.

Write

Write about: *Names for Body Parts*

Eyes can be called lookers.
Teeth can be called _____ .

Here are some words which can describe the five
body parts.

bright	keen	gentle	shining	dainty
rough	sharp	long	kind	ugly
powerful	smooth	strong	pointed	soft

Use some describing words for each of the five
body parts.

Write

Write about: *Describing Words for Body Parts*

Eyes can be called bright, shining lookers.
Teeth can be called _____ .

Think of other body parts and use describing
words of your own.

Before you write your story

Look at Kam's notebook.

This is how Kam used his notebook before he started to write his story about: *An Odd Man*

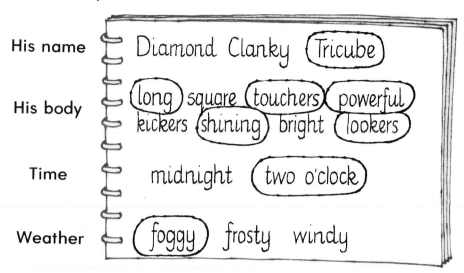

His name — Diamond Clanky (Tricube)

His body — (long) square (touchers) (powerful) kickers (shining) bright (lookers)

Time — midnight (two o'clock)

Weather — (foggy) frosty windy

Kam started his story in sentences, like this:

Tricube, the metal man, stretched out his long touchers and screwed on his powerful kickers. He switched on his shining lookers, turned his listeners into the hearing position and clanked off down the road. It was two o'clock on a foggy night . . .

Write your own story

If your *Odd Man* met another *Strange Creature*, you could call your writing: *Face to Face*

If your *Odd Man* walked along a road and found things which were *strange* to him, what might he try to do with them?

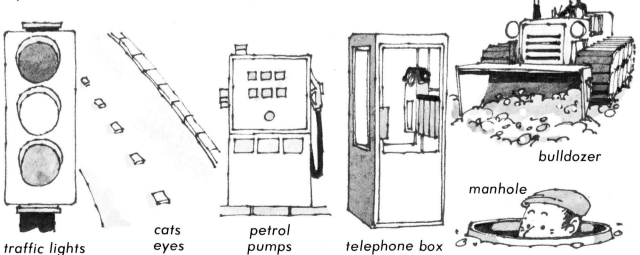

traffic lights

cats eyes

petrol pumps

telephone box

bulldozer

manhole

Fireworks and flashes

Remember,
Remember,
The fifth of November . . .

Freddie Firework says:

Firework Safety Rules

Keep a bucket of water ready.
Keep all pets indoors.
Keep a lid on your box of fireworks.
Keep a torch ready for reading instructions.
Keep away from fireworks when they are lit.

Remember... Remember... Teach your family the Firework Code.

Write

Draw the pictures and write the correct sentence by each one.

Never! Never! Never!

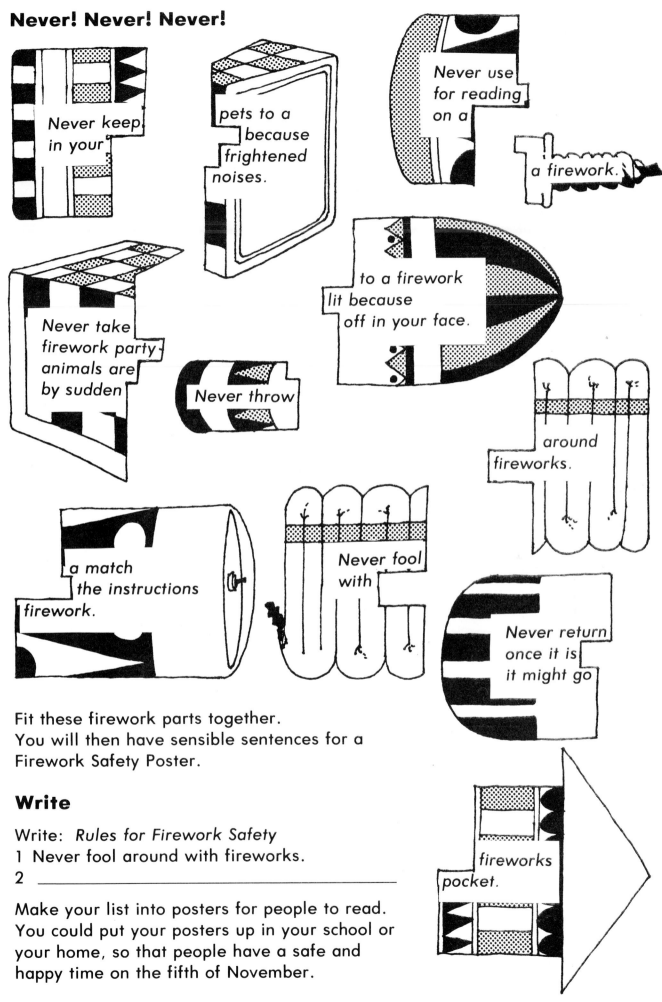

Never keep
in your

pets to a
because
frightened
noises.

Never use
for reading
on a

a firework.

Never take
firework party
animals are
by sudden

Never throw

to a firework
lit because
off in your face.

around
fireworks.

a match
the instructions
firework.

Never fool
with

Never return
once it is
it might go

fireworks
pocket.

Fit these firework parts together.
You will then have sensible sentences for a
Firework Safety Poster.

Write

Write: *Rules for Firework Safety*
1 Never fool around with fireworks.
2 _____

Make your list into posters for people to read.
You could put your posters up in your school or
your home, so that people have a safe and
happy time on the fifth of November.

The Magic Lamp

There was once a wizard who pretended to be the uncle of a boy called Aladdin. 'Come with me, dear nephew,' he said, 'and I will make you rich.' Aladdin was taken to a trap door which led to a cave under the ground. The wizard said, 'Climb down. Walk along the path until you come to a shelf in the rocks. There, on the shelf, you will see a small, shining lamp which is lit by oil. Bring it to me here.' Aladdin did as the wizard said, but when he returned to the trap door with the lamp, the wizard tried to snatch it from him.

'Help me out first,' cried Aladdin.

'Not likely!' shouted the wizard, and he banged the trap door shut above Aladdin's head.

'Let me out! Let me out!' yelled Aladdin.

Nobody heard. Nobody came.

There was Aladdin, all alone under the trap door. Big tears fell from his eyes. Plop! Plop! Plop! Some of Aladdin's tears fell onto the little lamp. Sadly he rubbed the tears off the lamp with his sleeve.

SSS! ZOOM! WHIZZ! BANG! WH-SSS!

It sounded like all the fireworks at a giant firework display going off.

Out of the flames, just like magic, stepped **The Magician of the Lamp.**

Read these colour phrases:

as green as grass	as white as snow
as red as fire	as bright as diamonds
	as blue as sapphires

Write

Write your own story about *A Magician*.
You could use some of the colour phrases to describe the Magician's eyes, hair, clothes and jewellery.

Shining Things

I love all shining things —
    The lovely moon
The silver stars at night,
    gold sun at noon.
A glowing rainbow in
    a stormy sky,
Or bright clouds hurrying
    when wind goes by.

Elizabeth Gould

Write

Sort these words into two sets.

silver	flowers	tinsel	dewdrops
stars	paintbox	patchwork	butterfly wings

Write the names of shining things in a sun shape.

Write the names of many coloured things
in a butterfly's wings.

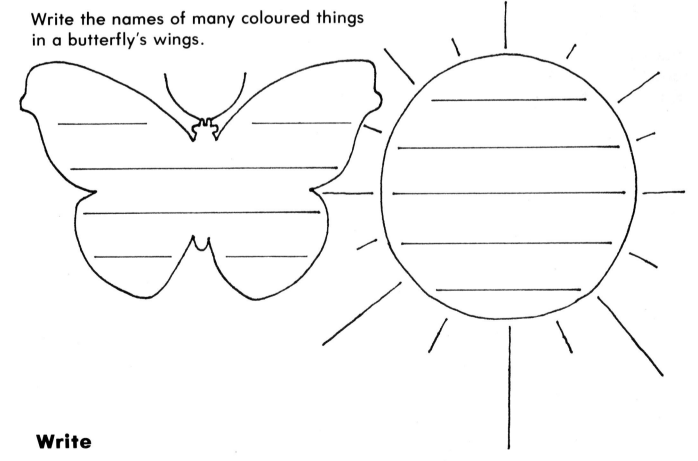

Write

Write a poem or short piece about: *Many Coloured Things*

All kinds of weather

In the Fog

Stand still.
The fog wraps you up
   and no-one can find you.

Walk.
The fog opens up
   to let you through
   and closes behind you.

Lilian Moore

Think about the difference between quiet fog and a noisy storm.

The quiet fog wraps you up and hides you.

The noisy storm tugs at your clothes,
smacks at your face and pushes you around.

Would you rather be out in the fog or out in a storm?

Write

Write a short piece about: *A Walk in the Fog*
or: *A Walk in a Storm*

When you read this poem, think about why the
poet has compared the movements of fog with
the movements of a cat.

The Fog

The fog comes
on little cat feet.
It sits looking
    over harbour and city
on silent haunches
and then moves on.

Carl Sandburg

When Carl Sandburg matched the movements of
fog with the movements of a cat, he made **an image.**

Think about

Think about the tap-tap-tapping of a drum.
Think about icing sugar falling softly onto a cake.
Think about a bull roaring and rampaging across a field.
Think about the swish-swishing sound of a broom
sweeping leaves.

Now think about the words:

snow	rain	storm	breeze

Match each weather word with a picture in your mind
and make your own **image.**

Write your own poem

Write poems about different kinds of weather.

What images do you have when you look at **the sky line at night?**

The Kingdom of Greyland

Every day King Greybeard went to the palace window, pulled back the grey curtains and looked out onto the grey gardens. 'Why is everything in my Kingdom so dull?' he said to himself. The King pulled on his bell cord and his Wise Man came into the room.

'Come and look at my Kingdom,' commanded the King. 'I can see beautiful shapes and patterns everywhere and yet I feel that there is something missing. Tell me why it looks so dull.'

The Wise Man replied,' The Kingdom of Greyland is dull, Your Majesty, because there are no colours in it.'

'Colours?' asked the King. 'What are colours?'

The Wise Man thought for a long time and then he said, 'I cannot explain what a colour is because you have never seen one. But I can tell you this — if the Kingdom of Greyland had colours in it, you could call it Rainbow Land.'

'I like the sound of Rainbow Land,' said the King. 'Order me some colours at once and I will have Greyland changed into Rainbow Land straight away.'

The Wise Man shook his head. 'Colours cannot be ordered,' he said. 'They don't just happen straight away. I can't explain because I'm not a painter.'

'Painter?' asked the King. 'What is a painter?'

'Ah! I can explain that,' replied the Wise Man. 'A painter is someone who goes round painting everything in **bright** colours.'

'Why didn't you say so before?' said the King a little more cheerfully. 'Go and find me a painter at once. Get one from another Kingdom if there isn't one in Greyland. Do it at once.'

So off went the Wise Man to find a painter.

The kingdom was *dull* because there were no colours in it, so the king called for a painter to come and make everything *bright*.

Write

Sort these words into two sets.

| grey | shining | dull | colourful | dismal | gloomy |
| gay | bright | dreary | brilliant | sparkling | colourless |

Write the words which mean *dull* in a cloud shape.
Write the words which mean *bright* in a star shape.

Shapes and patterns
Find: round, oval, star, feathery, spiky, curly shapes and patterns in this flower border.

Make a colourful picture of a rainbow.

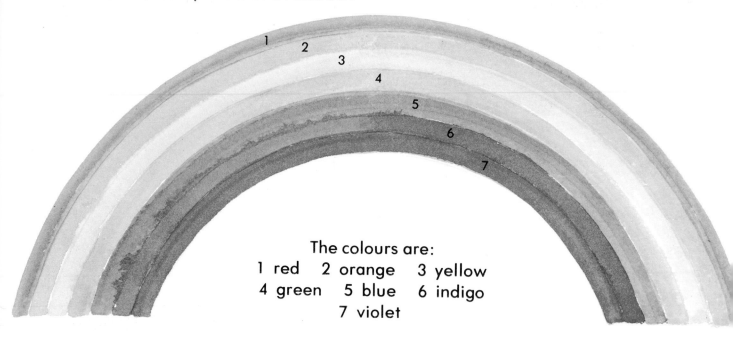

The colours are:
1 red   2 orange   3 yellow
4 green   5 blue   6 indigo
7 violet

Think about

Think about good ways to begin a story.
Here are two beginning parts:

The King's Painter

Far, far away, on the edge of a high cliff, stood
a tiny Fisherman's cottage.
An artist, called Peter, lived in the cottage.
or:
Deep, deep in a dark forest, many miles from the
nearest town, was a poor woodcutter's cottage.
An artist, called Peter, lived in the cottage.

Here is a following part:

Peter painted beautiful pictures of every colour
of the rainbow. Sometimes he felt sad because
no-one came to see his lovely, colourful work.

Think about what happened when the Wise Man
knocked on Peter's door.
How did Peter change Greyland to Rainbow Land?

Write your own story

You could begin your story with the parts you have
chosen, *or you could make up your own beginning
parts for a story called:* The King's Painter

Christmas

Just suppose . . . you received a letter with
one of these stamps
on the envelope . . .

and when you opened the envelope there was a
letter inside like this . . .

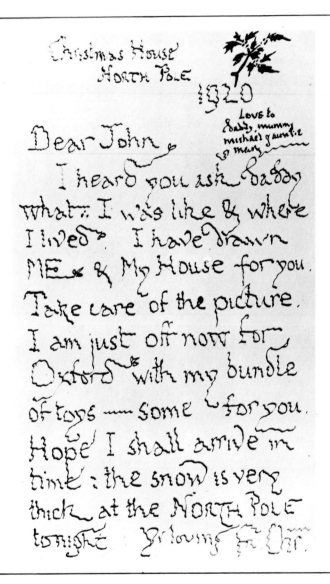

Father Christmas's handwriting was so shaky that
he had to have an Elf to be his secretary.
If you can read Father Christmas's shaky
handwriting, then you can be his secretary.

Write

Write out Father Christmas's letter in your own
strong, clear writing.

In a book called *The Father Christmas Letters*, you can read all about Father Christmas's helpers.

Father Christmas's chief assistant was North Polar Bear.
North Polar Bear made a great many muddles and troubles.

North Polar Bear
sets out to help

but . . .

Here are some more of
North Polar Bear's Muddles and Troubles

North Polar Bear let off a firework that turned the North Pole black and shook all the stars out of place.
He muddled up all the Christmas stockings.
When he went to the Cracker Hole, he dropped his candle onto the boxes of crackers and set his fur coat alight.
He fell down the tree he was decorating and got caught in the branches so that he looked like a decoration.
He fell through the roof of Father Christmas's house and made such a big hole that the snow fell in and spoilt the presents.
He cut his paw and he broke his leg *just* as the busy time began.

North Polar Bear
falls downstairs when
he tries to carry too
many presents.

North Polar Bear
goes to sleep when he
tries out too many of
the food parcels.

Write

Make a comic picture story **zig-zag** about:
North Polar Bear's Muddles and Troubles

Write a sentence for each picture.

This is how Father Christmas uses his notebook
before he starts to write his letters.

Ideas for North Pole stamps

Ideas for North Pole addresses

Ideas for decorations and pictures

How the Post Office likes
envelopes to be addressed

Imagine that you are Father Christmas and write a
letter to your family

Before you write your letter

Think who you will have for your chief assistant.

North Polar Bear   or   *Reindeer*   or   *Seal*   or   *Penguin*

Remember! You are Father Christmas.

Write your own letter

Write to your family about life at the North Pole.
Begin by writing your North Pole address at the top of your paper.
End by signing yourself *F. Christmas.*
Decorate your letter.
Put your letter in an envelope and address it to your family.
Draw a North Pole stamp on the envelope.
Take your letter home for your family to read.

A Walk in the Dark

Jonathan and the big iron pot were going up the side of Hemlock Mountain.

Now it was really beginning to be dark. Jonathan knew he should hurry, but the iron pot was heavy. Jonathan's steps were heavy and slow.

It was really and truly dark. The tall trees were dark. The woods were dark and scary.

'Crack!' a branch broke in the woods. It was as loud as a pistol shot. 'Woo-ooh. Wooooh!' That was an owl, but it was a most lonely sound.

Jonathan began to think about bears. And to keep up his courage he said, in time to his own slow steps:

There . . . are . . . no . . . bears . . . on . . . Hemlock . . . Mountain.
No bears . . . no . . . bears . . . at . . . all.

He was tired and out of breath. So he rested for a minute, then he went on saying:

There . . . are . . . no . . . bears . . . on . . . Hemlock . . . Mountain
No bears . . .

Watch out, Jonathan. Watch out! What was that, among the trees, right on top of the mountain? Two big, dark . . . what could they be?

Jonathan had to think quickly. There was only one thing to be done. Jonathan did it. He put the big iron pot upside down on the snow. Then he dug out a place and crawled under it.

The pot was like a safe house. Jonathan dug out another little place in the snow so that he could breathe.

Then he waited.

Go to a library and try to find a book called: *The Bears on Hemlock Mountain* by Alice Dagliesh. You can then read more about Jonathan.

These words describe different sounds:

Tap!   Bang!   Snap!   Growl!   Twitter!   Crunch!

These phrases give the meanings of the different sounds:

a soft sound made by a gentle knock

a sudden, loud noise

a small, trembling sound

a deep, murmuring sound

a sound of something being crushed

a quick, sharp sound

Write

Write each sound and its meaning.
Begin like this:

Bang! This is a sudden, loud noise.

This description gives, a scary feeling:

Two big, dark __eyes__ peered out from the
bushes.
They moved __slowly__ towards me.
They came __closer__ and __closer__ and __closer__.

Write

Make up a scary description of your own by writing the three sentences and changing the words in the spaces.

You could use some of these words:

cautiously   nearer   faces   creatures   quickly   faster

Before you write your story

Look at Kam's notebook.

This is how Kam used his notebook before he started to write his story about a walk in the dark.

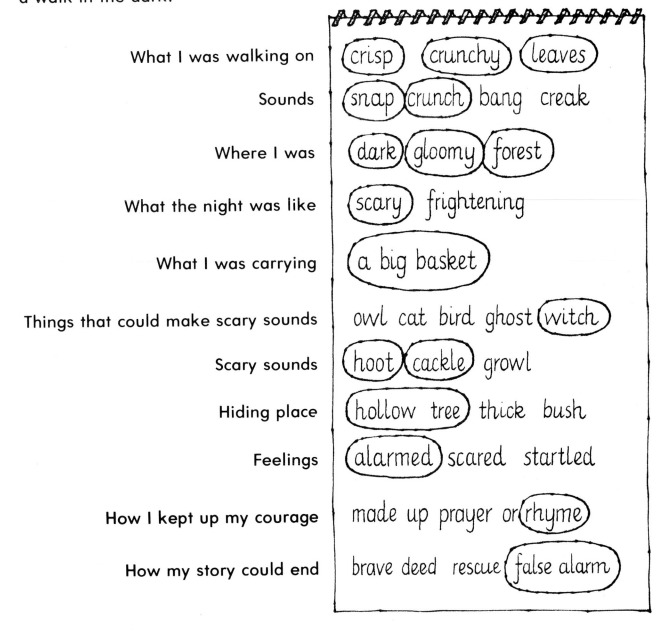

What I was walking on	(crisp) (crunchy) (leaves)
Sounds	(snap) (crunch) bang creak
Where I was	(dark) (gloomy) (forest)
What the night was like	(scary) frightening
What I was carrying	(a big basket)
Things that could make scary sounds	owl cat bird ghost (witch)
Scary sounds	(hoot) (cackle) growl
Hiding place	(hollow tree) thick bush
Feelings	(alarmed) scared startled
How I kept up my courage	made up prayer or (rhyme)
How my story could end	brave deed rescue (false alarm)

Look at Kam's ringed words.

Write your own story

You could call your writing: *A Walk in the Dark*.
You could begin by writing the sounds made by your feet.
Go on writing your story in complete sentences.

Country creatures

Read this information about two country creatures.

The hedgehog has a coat of prickles called spines. These spines grow on its head and back. There is rough, brown fur on the underside of its body.

Its tail is short and stumpy.

It has strong jaws and sharp teeth.

The hedgehog eats insects, grubs, slugs, worms and snails.

The hedgehog's senses of smell and hearing are very good, but it cannot see very well.

It makes its nest in a hollow in the ground, or in an old rabbit hole.

It goes out in the evening to hunt for food. It sleeps during the winter.

When there is danger, it curls up into a round, spiky ball for protection.

The red squirrel has a thick, reddish-brown fur coat. The underside of its body is covered with soft, white fur.

Its tail, which is long and fluffy, curls over its back and can be wrapped round its body for warmth on cold days.

The squirrel has strong, pointed teeth for gnawing its food. It eats berries, all kinds of nuts and sometimes birds' eggs.

It has very good sight and hearing, but a poor sense of smell.

Sometimes a squirrel uses an old bird's nest, or a hollow branch for its home high in a tree.

A squirrel goes out during the day time. It sleeps on cold winter days, but wakes up when the sun comes out.

Write

Look at this:

Make your own:

Collection box of information for the Hedgehog	Collection box of information for the Red Squirrel
coat prickles called spines on head and back	**coat**
tail short, stumpy	**tail**
teeth sharp strong jaws	**teeth**
food insects, grubs, slugs, worms	**food**
senses 1 sight — fair 2 smell — very good 3 hearing — very good	**senses** 1 sight — 2 smell — 3 hearing —
home nest in hollow old rabbit hole	**home**
behaviour out at night sleeps in winter curls up in a ball when in danger	**behaviour**

Write

Write about: *How to tell the difference between a Hedgehog and a Red Squirrel*

Remember to describe all the tiny details when you write.
Do not write: The hedgehog has a tail.
Write: The hedgehog has a short, stumpy tail.

Remember to show the differences when you write.
Write: The hedgehog has a short, stumpy tail, but the red squirrel has a long, fluffy tail.

What in the world?

Read the first verse of this **riddle poem** and try
to guess the answer.

> What in the world
>   goes whiskery friskery
>   meowling and prowling
>   napping and lapping
>   at silky milk?
>
> Psst
> What is it?

Eve Merriman

Read the poem again and as you read decide
which words give you the best clues to the
answer: CAT.

Write

Write the clue words from the poem close
together and then draw a cat shape round them
like this:

whiskery friskery
meowling prowling
napping lapping
silky milk

Write

Write these two sets of clue words.
Draw the shape of the answer round each set.

piggery wiggery
grunting shunting
gobbling scrobbling
slushy wushy
mush

wriggling wiggling sliding gliding squirming worming squishy squashy mud

Write

Write the first two verses of your own *What in the World?* poem.

34

Now read another verse of Eve Merriman's poem
and guess again.

> What in the world
>   goes gnawing and pawing
>   scratching and latching
>   sniffing and squiffing
>   nibbling for tidbits of left-over cheese?
>
> Please?!

Read the poem again and decide which words
give you the clues to the answer: MOUSE.

Notice that a strange word for a mouse has been
used: squiffing. We know that mice go sniffing
about, but not squiffing.
The poet has written 'sniffing and squiffing',
because the two words *sound* well together.

Say these sets of words quietly to yourself:

blinkery	winkery
tuwhitting	tuwhooing
staring	glaring
swooping	scooping

barking	larking
snuffling	wuffling
snapping	yapping
growling	prowling

Write

Make each set of words into a verse.
Add these verses to your *What in the World?* poem.

Now collect your own set of words for another verse.

Remember that you can use 'make up' words if they sound well together.

Add this verse to your *What in the World?* poem.

You can add more verses to your poem.

You never can tell

The first words of a story from Iceland are:

When you wake up in the morning
you never can tell what might happen to you
during the day.

The story goes on:

One fine morning Prince Lini woke up in his
castle on the hill. He didn't have the slightest
idea what was going to happen to him that day.

He rode into the forest with his friends.

Suddenly, from nowhere, a thick fog blew into
the woods. The cloud of fog covered the prince
from head to toe.

A minute later the fog drifted away and was
gone. Gone, too, was Prince Lini.

Think about who could have taken Prince Lini away.

A white swan

A wicked troll

*The King of the
Weather Storms*

In the story, the Prince's friends search for him.
The Prince's father, the King, says:

*Whoever finds
Prince Lini and
brings him back to me
will win half of
my kingdom.*

Eventually Prince Lini is found by a girl called Signy.

Think about

Think about: where Signy could have found Prince Lini;
how she managed to rescue him;
what the King gave her as her reward;
what happened after that.

Write your own story

You could write about: *The Prince who was Lost*
or:
read the last words of the story from Iceland
which say:

When you wake up in the morning —
tomorrow morning —
you never can tell what might happen to *you*
during the day.

and write about: *What happened to me
during that strange day.*

Faces

Faces can show how people **feel.**
Look at the pictures and see if you can find:
a **happy** face; a **sad** face; a **surprised** face;
an **angry** face.

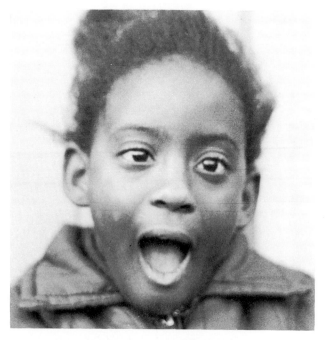 

Look again at the pictures and match each face
with one of the sentences.

'I feel astonished and amazed.'
'I feel pleased and contented.'
'I feel sorrowful and mournful.'
'I feel displeased and annoyed.'

Look again at the **first** picture.
Look at the way in which the girl's open mouth
shows **astonishment.**
Look at the way in which she is rolling her eyes
in **amazement.**

What could happen to give **your face** an
expression of surprise?

Write

Write a short piece about: *My Face*
You could begin by writing:

I had an expression of surprise on my face when . . .
I had an expression of anger when . . .
I had an expression of pleasure when . . .
I had an expression of sadness when . . .

Look at Sharon's *Self Portrait* and read her
description of herself.

The Real Me
I have a roundish face, a
litte nose and brown eyes.
The expression on my face
is very serious. My dad says
I look a bit miserable, that's
because I am thinking.
You can see that by the
little lines on my
forehead.

Look at yourself in a mirror.
Draw a picture of yourself. Look at your self
portrait and decide whether your face tells about
the real you.

Write

Write a piece called: *The Real Me*

The Wicked One

Read these three sentences which begin a story called *Baba Yaga*.

Once upon a time, far far away in dense and dark woods, there lived a terrible witch called Baba Yaga.

Her hut stood on two giant chicken legs and was surrounded by human bones and skulls with a flame burning inside each one . . .

When she went out Baba Yaga travelled in a mortar, a huge bowl that made a terrible noise.

Write

Write these sentences with the correct endings from the Baba Yaga story.

All this happened . . . deep, deep down in a musty, dusty cave.
far, far away in dense and dark woods.
long, long ago in a kingdom over the sea.

There lived a . . . demon queen called Rotti Grotti.
horrible goblin called Pinchi Punchi.
terrible witch called Baba Yaga.

Her home was . . . a creepy castle covered with cobwebs.
a hut standing on two giant chicken legs.
the empty shell of a dead crab.

She moved around in . . . an old grandfather clock.
a large tin kettle.
a huge bowl.

People heard her coming because . . . the kettle made a whistling noise.
the grandfather clock made a chiming noise.
the bowl made a terrible noise.

People knew when Baba Yaga was coming because they heard a terrible noise.

But people didn't know where Baba Yaga had come from because something, **guided by invisible hands,** travelled behind her and swept away all traces of her journey. What could it be?

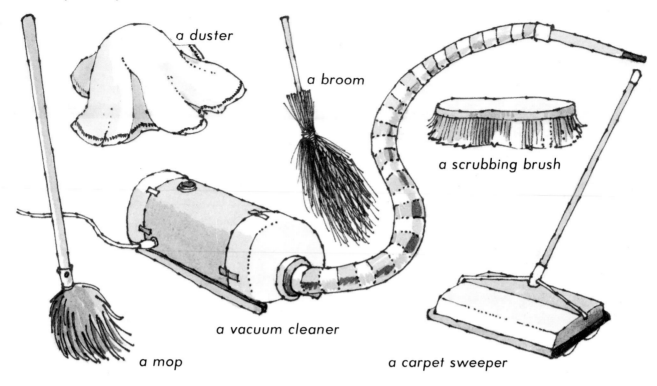

a duster

a broom

a scrubbing brush

a vacuum cleaner

a mop

a carpet sweeper

It was a ⌐broom⌐ (shown reversed/upside down in box)

Read all the sentence endings on page 40 again.
Find a set of sentences which could tell about Rotti Grotti, the demon queen.

Write

Call your writing: *Rotti Grotti the Demon Queen*
Begin:

Long, long ago, in a kingdom over the sea, there lived a demon queen called Rotti Grotti. Her home . . .

Find another set of sentences for the beginning of a story about Pinchi Punchi.
Call your writing: *Pinchi Punchi the Horrible Goblin*
Begin:
Deep, deep down . . .

Write your own story

You could call your writing: *The Wicked One*
Will you have a witch, a demon queen, a horrible goblin, or . . .
to be the wicked one in your story?

Talking with pictures

Paul is in a hospital school. He cannot move his legs and arms properly, but he can point with his helmet pointer.

Paul can see and hear, but he cannot speak.

When Paul wants to give a message, he points to a picture on his picture chart. The pictures on Paul's chart are called **Symbols.**

Here are some of the symbols on Paul's chart.

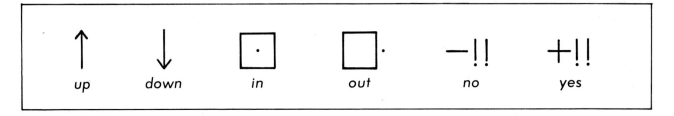

Here are some symbols for **Parts of the Body.**

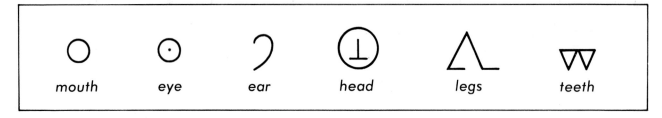

This symbol means **I** or **Me.** ⊥| This symbol means **Pain.** ♡⌒

These three symbols mean: **I pain ear**
The sentence for the three symbols is:
I have a pain in my ear.

Write

Write the meanings of these sets of symbols in complete sentences.

Here are some more symbols from Paul's chart.

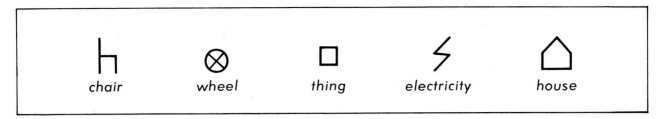

| chair | wheel | thing | electricity | house |

Make up your own symbols for the following
and put them between these marks: Ⓞ   Ⓞ

| a table | a bed | a boat | a fire | a car | an aeroplane |

| a book for reading | a picture dictionary | a television set |

Number each symbol.
Ask your friends to say what each of your symbols means.
You have made a good symbol if your friends can guess the meaning
at once.

Some symbols are put together on Paul's chart.

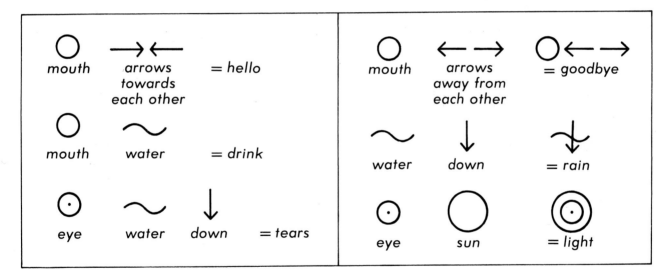

Write

These symbols are on Paul's chart.
Write what each set of symbols means to you.

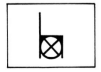 The chair and the wheel together could mean . . .

  A wheel with wings could mean . . .

  Two wheels with something to guide them could mean . . .

  A house with two wheels could mean . . .

It is difficult to draw a picture about how someone feels.

A heart shape ♡ is Paul's symbol for **feelings.**

These symbols from Paul's chart show feelings.

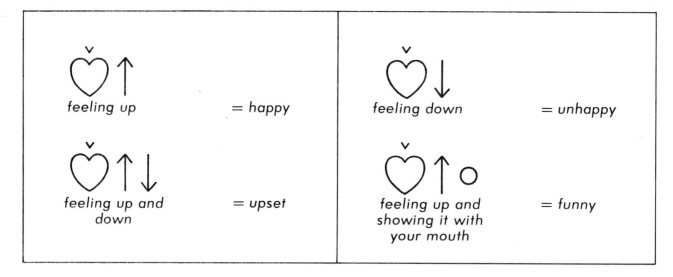

feeling up = happy	feeling down = unhappy
feeling up and down = upset	feeling up and showing it with your mouth = funny

Imagine that you visit Paul. Then you write about your visit because you want your friends to know how much you and Paul enjoyed it.

Think about

Think about what you say to Paul when you sit by his chair. Which symbol would he point to you in reply?

Think about some of the things you could do to make him laugh. Could you make funny faces? Could you make up a guessing game and use the picture chart for his answers?

You could point to ⊠ and, □⊙⊃∫ and then he would know that you would push his wheelchair over to the television set.

Think about the television programme you would watch together. Which parts of the programme might you **both** enjoy most?

Write

Write about: *A Visit to Paul's School*

Don't forget to say ○ ← → before you go home.

The hot hatful

Anansi the Spider Man and the Hot Hatful

Some parts of this picture story are missing.

A gentle breeze carried the smell out of the kitchen and over to Anansi.

Anansi thought that he would _____ _____ _____

'No-one must see me with this hat full of hot rice and peas,' he said.

Guess what happened in the missing picture. What do you think Anansi did after he smelt the delicious peas and rice cooking in the pot?

The birds _____ _____ _____ _____

He panicked. In desperation he put the hatful of rice and peas on his head.

Poor Anansi _____ _____ _____ _____

Why were the birds so attracted to Anansi's hat? What could have happened to Anansi's head when he put the hot hatful of peas and rice on it? Guess what happened in the missing picture.

Write

Write a complete story called: *Anansi's Hot Hatful*

Friends

Read these three story parts.
Each of the three story parts is called a **paragraph.**

Once there were three friends.
The first spent much of its time in the air.
The second enjoyed life on the water.
The third lived under the ground.
But each day the three friends met together to
talk about the things they knew best.

   The one who flew about in the air knew a
great deal about what was happening in the
world down below.
The one who enjoyed life on the water saw very
little beyond the river bank and swam up and
down listening to water sounds.
The one who lived underground just worked
away, mostly in the darkness and had no worries
about the weather.

   The three friends delighted in each other's
company and spent many happy hours talking
about the things they knew best.
And, like all good friends, they always helped
each other out in times of trouble.

Can you guess what **kind** of creature each of the
three friends was?

Read the names of all the creatures in the box.

bat	bird	bee	duck	fly	water rat
turtle	worm	mole	shrew	mouse	otter

Write

Write these three headings and put each creature under the correct one.

In the Air	On the Water	Under the Ground

Put a ring round one creature in each list which you would like to have in your story.

Write a sentence which tells about something interesting **your** air creature saw.

Write **another** sentence about your air creature beginning:

'As I looked down on the world, I said to myself, _____'

Write a sentence about something **your** water creature saw as it swam.

Write **another** sentence beginning:

'As I floated gently down stream, I thought, _____'

Write a sentence about something **your** underground creature heard.

Write **another** sentence beginning:

'As I scraped my way up to the fresh air, I kept wishing that _____'

Think of the times of trouble which **your** three friends might have had.

Write these three headings and put the troubles under each one.

Weather	Food	Enemies
snow storm	too little food	fox
flood	no water	man

Add more troubles for your own creatures.

Write your own story

You could call your writing: *The Three Friends*

47

Making a choice

PIRATES' POP INN

OPEN 11·30 - 21 hrs

PIRATES' PLATTERS

Beefburger and chips

Sausages and baked beans

Fish fingers and chips

PIRATES' PUDDINGS

Ice cream with chocolate sauce.

Jam roll with custard.

PICK YOUR POP

Glass of :

cola

orange

grapefruit

THE WHISTLING KETTLE CAFE

LIGHT SNACKS
(Served at all times)

Poached egg on toast

o

Sausages (2) and beans

o

Scrambled egg on toast

LUNCH OF THE DAY
(12 noon - 14 hrs)

Soup

o

Roast beef with potatoes and peas

o

Fruit salad

o

Coffee

SUPPER MENU
(18 hrs - 22 hrs)

Soup

o

Sausage and mash

or

Beefburger and beans

or

Fish fingers and chips

Ice cream

Tea or coffee

Write

Call your writing: *Choosing My Favourite Foods*

Read the menu card outside The Pirates' Pop Inn.
Decide which is your favourite platter.
Write a sentence about your choice.

Look at the list of Pirates' Puddings.
Decide which is your favourite pudding.
Write a sentence about your choice.

Look at the list of drinks.
Decide which is your favourite drink.
Write a sentence about your choice.

Read the menu card outside The Whistling Kettle Café.
Write these sentence beginnings and then complete them.

If I went to The Whistling Kettle Café at 10.30 in the morning,
I would choose_____.

If I went to The Whistling Kettle Café at 14.00 hrs,
I would choose_____.

If I went to The Whistling Kettle Café at 12.30,
I would choose_____.

If I went to The Whistling Kettle Café at 20.00 hrs,
I would choose_____.

If you could go to only one Café, decide which
you would choose and what time you would go.

Write a short piece about: *A Meal at_____*

Write your own menu card

Write a menu card of your favourite foods.

My Perfect Menu

Thinking about food

Do you sometimes sit and think about food?

A long time ago, men lived in caves and hunted wild animals for food. Sometimes, before they went hunting, they would draw pictures on the walls of their caves of the animals they hoped to catch. They hoped that thinking about the animals in this way would bring them good luck in their hunting.

Here is a **picture in words** of food.

This food is cold, sweet to taste and very slippery. Sometimes it comes in a rectangular block, sometimes in a tub and sometimes in a cone. It can be many flavours such as strawberry, chocolate or vanilla.

Write

Write some **Food Riddles** and try them out on your friends.

These words can be used to describe food.

greasy	bright	cold	smooth	dull	sizzling	crunchy
fizzy	sticky	colourful	crackling	sweet	juicy	
bitter	salty	sour	bubbling	hot	fishy	soggy

You can use your **five senses** to describe food.

Write

Call your writing: *All About Food*
Write these five headings. Put each word from
the box above underneath the **sense** or **senses**
which you could use to describe it.

sight	**hearing**	**taste**	**smell**	**touch**

Add some more describing words of your own.

Imagine you met someone from another country
who had never eaten these foods.

bacon and eggs   *treacle pudding*   *sausage and chips*

Write a short piece describing each one.

All these foods are eaten by people in different
parts of the world.

Egg Noodles	Toad in the Hole
Frogs' Legs	Snails
Yams	Sharks' Fins
Kangaroo Soup	Shepherd's Pie

Write a short piece describing **one** food which
you have tasted.
Imagine what each one tastes like even if you
have never eaten any.
Write a sentence about how you imagine each
food tastes.

Read Part One of this *Danny Fox* story.

Danny Fox lived in a small cave on the side of a mountain near the sea. He had a wife called Doxie and three children who were always hungry. Danny and Doxie were often hungry too. The names of their children were Lick, Chew, and Swallow . . .

One day the little foxes woke up early and began to whine and yelp and howl. 'Oh please fetch some food,' said Mrs Doxie Fox. 'Lick, Chew and Swallow need something to lick, chew and swallow, and I need something too.' Danny Fox sat up and yawned . . . Then he put his nose outside the cave and sniffed the cold air. 'Sniff, sniff. I can sniff a rabbit.' He began to run faster and faster up the mountainside, sniffing the ground. Then he saw the rabbit, and yelped and ran faster than ever. But the rabbit escaped by diving into a crack between two rocks. The crack was too narrow for Danny . . .

So Danny Fox had no luck with the rabbit.

In Part Two, Danny Fox still had no luck.
The story goes on:

'Sniff, sniff. I can sniff a pigeon.' But . . .
'Sniff, sniff. I can smell a mouse.' But . . .
'Sniff, sniff. I can smell a duck.' But . . .
'Sniff, sniff. I can smell a goose.' But . . .

What do you think happened each time Danny Fox was unlucky?

Write

Write the whole of Part Two of the *Danny Fox* story yourself.
You could call your writing: *Danny Fox has an Unlucky Morning*

Part Three of the *Danny Fox* story is left out.

Now read Part Four.

So Danny and Doxie and Lick and Chew and Swallow had an enormous feast. They ate and they ate until they could eat no more. Then they all fell down together in a heap, fast asleep.

So Danny Fox's unlucky morning must have changed to a lucky afternoon.

Before you write part three

Think about what might have happened to change Danny's luck in Part Three of the story.

How did Danny manage to find food for 'an enormous feast' for his family?

Where did he go?

What kind of smell did he sniff? Was it . . .

fish

or eggs

or a cock

or . . . ?

Was he in danger?
If so, was his enemy . . .

a fisherman

or a policeman

or a farmer

or . . . ?

How did he escape?

How did he manage to carry enough food home for his family to eat and eat until 'they could eat no more'?

What did the family say to each other as they enjoyed the feast?

Write your own part three

Write Part Three of the story yourself.
You could call your writing: *Danny Fox has a Lucky Afternoon*

Trouble in the Ark

In a book called *The Log of the Ark*, the captain is Noah, his ship is the Ark, and his passengers are the animals.

When the animals are inside the Ark, Hippopotamus says:

'We're on The Ark
What a lark!'

But then Noah's troubles begin.
Noah says:

'Now . . . stop swinging your trunk around.'

'I can't take the roof off the Ark, so you will just have to curl your long neck up . . .'

'Please . . ., let that poor little creature use your hump for a cushion.'

Write

Call your writing: *Noah's Troubles*
You could begin by writing the sentences and filling in the missing names of the animals.

Write about some more troubles with other animals. Use the picture to help you.

Think about

Think about: *The First Night on the Ark*

Imagine the trouble over where each pair of animals sleeps!

Yak wants straw to sleep on, but Camel eats it.
What do you think they say to each other?

Imagine the trouble over the bath water!

Hippopotamus splashes so much that he almost drowns Rat.
Elephant looks as if he is drinking when he is squirting
water over his back.
What do the other animals say?

Imagine what it is like during that first night on board!

Some frightened creatures cry softly to themselves.
Some large, heavy snorers keep everyone awake.
Some night creatures, like Owl, don't want to sleep at all.
What does Noah say?

Imagine the trouble over breakfast next morning!

Hippopotamus wants melons.
Monkey wants nuts.
Nobody wants Mrs Noah's porridge.
What does Noah say?
What does Mrs Noah say?

Write

Write a piece about that first night on the Ark.
You could call your writing: *Bed and Breakfast on the Ark*

55

A Ship's **Log** is a kind of **Diary** in which the captain of the ship writes down everything that happens each day.

Here is a torn piece of Noah's Log after the first night on the Ark.

The Log of the Ark
What a terrible night! I only got one hour's sleep
from now on I am going to make big changes
Hedgehog must be moved away from
Never again will I let Ostrich
Porridge must always

Before you write your ship's log

Guess what Noah wrote about Hedgehog, Ostrich and the porridge.

Read these chapter headings from *The Log of the Ark*.
The headings could give you some ideas for your own writing.

Baths and Breakfast	Dirty Weather
The First Day on Board	The Concert
The Alarm in the Night	Land in Sight
The Elephant Chokes	Goodbyes

Write your own ship's log

You could call your writing: *The Log of the Ark — First Week*
or:
Make a diary booklet by folding over some pieces of paper.
Write: *The Log of the Ark* on the cover.
You could write the diary as if you are Noah, or Mrs Noah
or One of the Animals

In a book of poems called *Beasts' Choir*,
each voice tells God about its troubles.

Guess who is speaking:

> Lord,
> You try for a little while
> to walk on one foot
> carrying Your whole heaven
> on Your back.

> It's true
> I'm a little talkative
> but, at times,
> that is useful:
> heads are thick,
> slow to understand
> and have to be told things
> again and again . . .

> To have my name
> among the stars,
> then to think
> I may end as a bedside rug!
> Oh, Lord,
> this thought makes me
> terribly gruff . . .

Think about

Think about:

how a kangaroo feels about having a pouch
(when its babies start fighting)

how a giraffe feels about its long neck
(when it has a sore throat)

how . . .

Write your own poems

Write some poems called: *Animal Voices*

Picture poems and shape poems

Words can be put on a page so that they look like pictures of what they say.

Pictures of words are called **calligrams.**

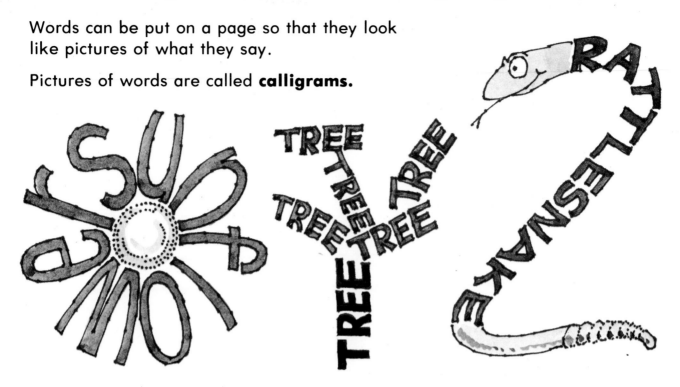

Here are some more ideas for calligrams.

Make up your own calligrams

Make up more calligrams of your own.
You could use some of these words.

spooky	shivery	candyfloss	crash
pop	twinkling	zoom	zig-zag
abracadabra	pitter-patter	lollipop	

The shape made by the words tells you what this poem is about.

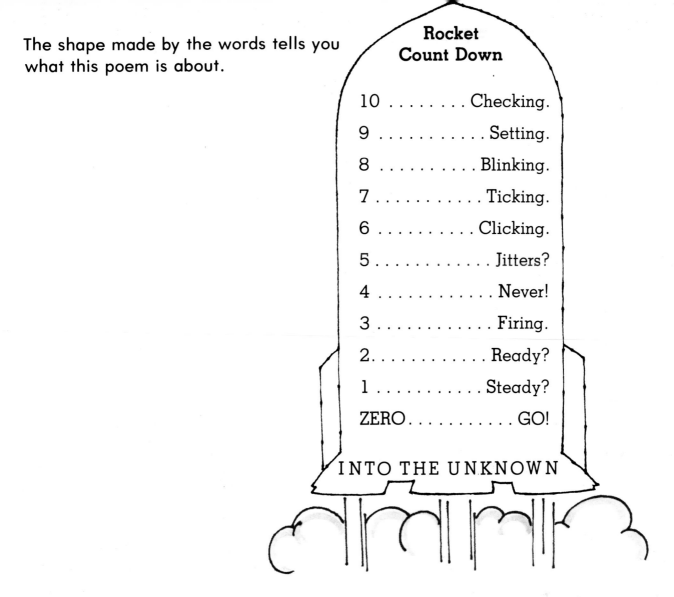

Rocket Count Down

10 . . . . Checking.

9 . . . . Setting.

8 . . . . Blinking.

7 . . . . Ticking.

6 . . . . Clicking.

5 . . . . Jitters?

4 . . . . Never!

3 . . . . Firing.

2 . . . . Ready?

1 . . . . Steady?

ZERO . . . . GO!

INTO THE UNKNOWN

Here is another idea for a Shape Poem.

Going up on the escalator

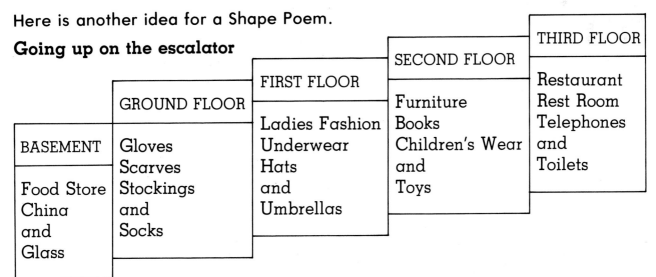

THIRD FLOOR
Restaurant Rest Room Telephones and Toilets

SECOND FLOOR
Furniture Books Children's Wear and Toys

FIRST FLOOR
Ladies Fashion Underwear Hats and Umbrellas

GROUND FLOOR
Gloves Scarves Stockings and Socks

BASEMENT
Food Store China and Glass

Write your own shape poem

You could call your poem: *Going Up*
or: *Going Down*
Make a collection of your own *Shape Poems*

Sail away

In a story book called *The Little Captain*, a boy sets sail in his brave ship *Never Sink*.

Put your finger on the brave ship *Never Sink*. Trace its voyage on the picture map.

Read these five short pieces and match each one with a place on the picture map.

The people of Popinjay looked like a lot of parrots, because they loved to dress in red and green and yellow clothes.

The Dragon Gates were made of stone at night, but at dawn they slowly came to life, first their tongues and then their heads.

There were trees as high as church steeples and flowers as big as sunshades and shells like tents.

The dead volcano was coming back to life. The earth shook and shuddered and heaved like the waves of the sea. Trees crashed to the ground and in the distance a fountain of hissing steam burst into the air.

Only a few lights glimmered through the fog like holes in a white sheet. Mostly the doors and windows were dark, so the whole town seemed shrouded in gloom.

Write

Write a short piece about: *Popinjay Port*.

Describe the girls' dresses and the boys' hats. Describe the curtains at the windows of the houses and the flags flying in the market place. Describe the market. What was bought and sold there? What were the people like?

Write a short piece about each of the other places.

The Dragon Gates: where the dragons slowly came to life — 'right down to the tips of their tails'. What did the dragons sound like?

A picture map of the voyage of *Never Sink*

60

The Mountain of Fire: which hissed and sizzled and shook.
What happened to the ships sailing in the nearby waters?
The Island of Evertaller: where everything was gigantic in size.
Did anyone live there?
The Misty City: which rose like a ghost on stilts out of the sea.
Was this a silent and empty place, or did someone or something live there?

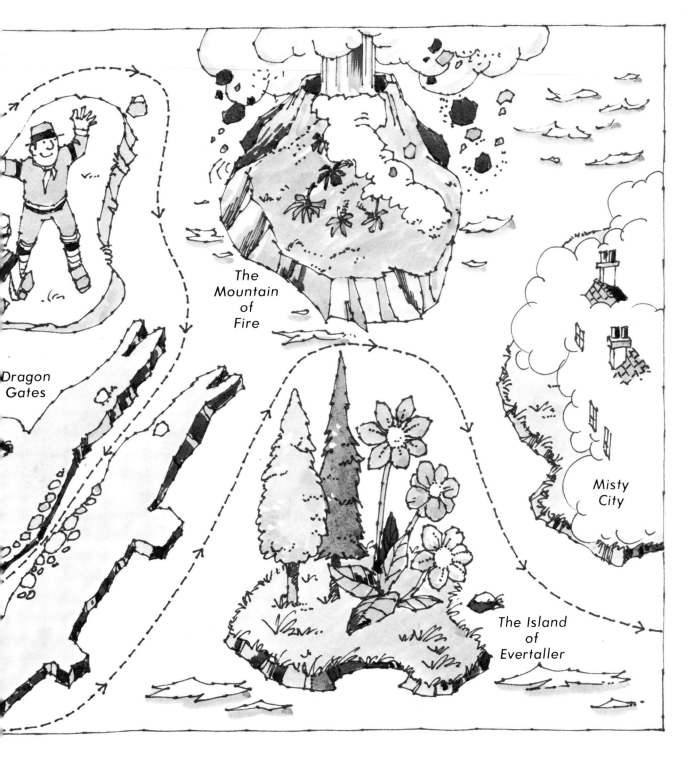

In the story book, the boy who is The Little Captain, sets sail with three companions. These companions are Podgy Plum, Marinka and Timid Thomas.

Guess which of the three companions says:

'D-do we have to go through b-big black gates in the d-dark?'

Notice how the story-writer makes Timid Thomas's words look frightened on the page.

Write

Write these sentences as if Timid Thomas were saying them in a frightened voice. Say the words to yourself as you write.
Call your writing: *Timid Thomas Talking*

'Don't make so much noise — there may be cannibals!'

'Oh no, for goodness' sake, that would be far too dangerous.'

'Boo hoo! What shall we do now?'

Write some **calligrams** for Timid Thomas.

Make **tremble** TREMBLE and **shiver** SHIVER
How many **scary** words can you write as **calligrams?**

Think about

Think about going on a voyage.
Choose some companions you would like to take with you.

a good cook   *a story teller*   *someone to make you laugh*   *a pet*

Write

Write a short piece about each of the companions you have chosen.
Say **why** you chose them.
You could call your writing: *My Companions for the Voyage*

Before you write your story

Draw a picture map for **your** voyage.

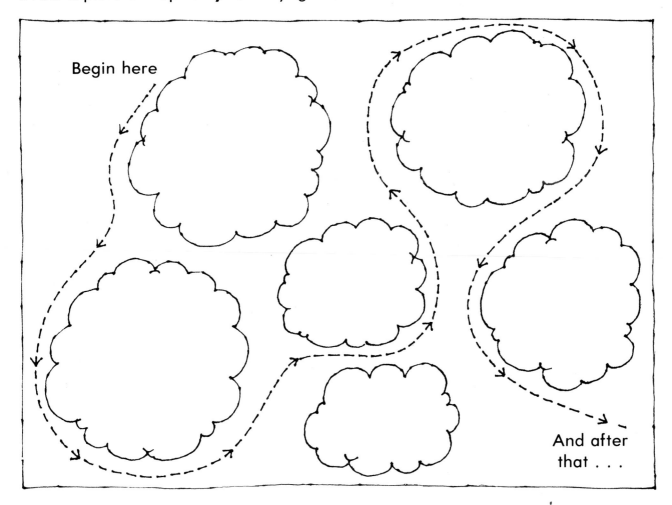

Begin here

And after that . . .

Fill in each cloud with a small picture of a special place on your route.
Give each place an exciting name.

Choose a name for your ship or craft.

Decide who you will have for your companions.

Will you have some terrifying adventures and then return to your home for ever? Or will you be like The Little Captain in the book?

The story ends:

'But as for the little captain . . . he will sail away again one of these days, for the world is full of islands and wonderful adventures.'

Write your own story

Write a long story called: *The Voyage of The Good Ship . . .*
or: *From Planet to Planet*

Acknowledgments

For permission to use copyright material acknowledgment is made to the following:

For the page of illustration from **The Magician and the Sorcerer** by David McKee to the illustrator and Abelard-Schuman Ltd; for *In the Fog* by Lilian Moore from **I Feel the Same Way** and *What in the World?* by Eve Merriman from **There is No Rhyme for Silver** used by permission of Atheneum Publishers; for the Blissymbolics used here © Blissymbolics Communication Institute 1979, Toronto, Canada; for the extract from **Baba Yaga** by Celine Leopold to the author and Bodley Head; for the extract from **The Little Captain** by Paul Biegel to the author and J.M. Dent and Sons Ltd; for *Shining Things* from **Come Follow Me** by Elizabeth Gould to the author and Evans Brothers Ltd; for the extract from Chapter 4 of **The Iron Man** by Ted Hughes to the author and reprinted by permission of Faber and Faber Ltd; for *Prince Lini* from **Half a Kingdom** by Ann McGovern to the author and Frederick Warne (Publishers) Ltd; for the Father Christmas letter from page 20 of **Father Christmas Letters** by J.R.R. Tolkien to the author and George Allen and Unwin (Publishers) Ltd; for *Fog* from **Chicago Poems** by Carl Sandburg, © 1916 by Holt, Rinehart and Winston, Inc, copyright 1944 by Carl Sandburg. Reprinted by permission of Harcourt, Brace, Jovanich Inc; for the extract from **The Log of the Ark** by Kenneth Walker to the estates of Kenneth Walker and Geoffrey Boumphrey and Jonathan Cape Ltd; for extracts from **Beasts' Choir** by Carmen de Gasztold, translated by Rumer Godden to the author, translater and Macmillan London and Basingstoke; for extracts from pages 9-20 of Danny Fox by David Thomson © David Thomson 1966 abridged with permission of Penguin Books Ltd.

Every effort has been made to trace owners of copyright material, but in some cases this has not proved possible. The publishers would be glad to hear from any further copyright owners of material reproduced in **Approaches to Writing and Language** Book 2.